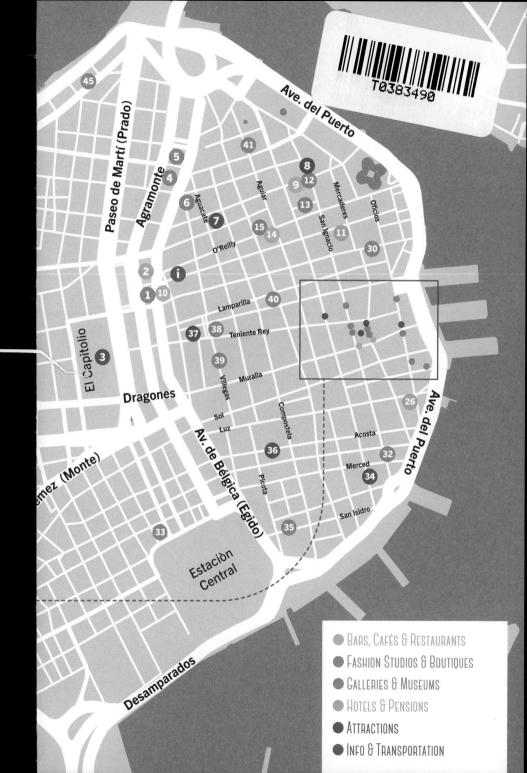

Bars, Cafés & Restaurants
Fashion Studios & Boutiques
Galleries & Museums
Hotels & Pensions
Attractions
Info & Transportation

T0383490

UPCYCLING
HAVANA

UPCYCLING HAVANA

Fashion, Art & Architecture

Edited by Boris Antonio Pérez Vázquez
and Michael M. Thoss

HIRMER

CONTENTS

PREFACE

WALK

FASHION

ARCHITECTURE

APPENDIX

CUBA'S CREATIVITY
OF SCARCITY

"Cuba may be lagging behind economically, but in this area we're at the fore-front," says a Havana fashion designer, referring to the clever and creative upcycling of used clothing that has spawned an alternative fashion industry in Havana. Seamstresses and designers have been joining forces more and more often, launching cutting-edge fashion brands and their own boutiques—if necessary, even operating out of their living rooms or gardens. Small businesses such as these, called *mipymes* in Cuba, are now an important force within an otherwise stagnant state economy badly scarred by six decades of the US embargo. Fashion and design in particular have taken on a life of their own, as Cuba, the largest island in the Caribbean, has a huge pent-up demand in these areas.

"Recycling out of necessity—that's something we know about from decades of living with scarcity. That's why the word 'recycling' didn't have such a good reputation here until recently. But that's all changing now," sums up one of the Havanan designers. Synthetic mass-produced "Made in China" stuff? Absolutely not cool! A new generation of fashion designers is forming in Havana, and they're inspired by sustainable lifestyle brands in the capitalist North just as they're familiar with trends in the global South: for them, Berlin, Milan, and New York are on a par with Lagos, Mumbai, and Rio. This goes hand in hand with the overall recycling attitude one finds in Havana, whether it be the refurbishment of buildings or the everyday habits of Cuban households.

In regard to fashion, "many of my students' creations revive our Afro-Cuban heritage and combine it with feminist and queer themes. You can also discover forms of resilience and aesthetic resistance in them," explains a young teacher at the State Institute of Industrial Design (ISDI). The new self-confidence of young Afro-Cubans is evident today not just in fashion but also music, hairstyles, and body art. Until very recently, much of Cuban fashion and style was dominated by white culture. In 1952, the retailer El Encanto became the first branch of the fashion house Dior in the Americas, as well as a favorite meeting spot for Hollywood stars. Following their victory, the Cuban revolutionaries transformed their country's fashion industry into unform factories, and they turned El Encanto, a world-famous luxury department store, into a warehouse that was then destroyed by arson in 1961. A similar fate befell the architecture of what was once the most modern city in Latin America, a place where all European architectural styles, from Spanish Baroque to Art Deco to the Bauhaus, were adopted and re- or upcycled into the "Eclecticismo" the country is known for.

Since 2012, Cuban fashion designers have again been permitted to work independently for themselves (a privilege still denied to Cuban architects and gallerists). As concerns their working conditions, they can be seen as already part of our global future: increasing shortages of resources, the fallout from climate change, and the polluting of our planet all inform their creations. Hence their term for an enduring circular economy: "Recycling, Repair, Recommerce." As far as they're concerned, excessive haute couture and unethical fast fashion belong in the dustbin of history. Turning away from wasteful commercial clothing, their upcycled one-offs and ephemeral sculptures of the body have transformed Havana into the longest and wildest catwalk in the Caribbean.

With this very personal book, we invite you to accompany some of them and their models to hip bars, boutiques, hotels, art galleries, and hidden places—to experience Havana in a completely new way, not like the usual tourist. So join us on a walk through the city and enjoy these carefully selected, unusual, unexpected, and unforgettable places. Over the course of a two- or three-day visit to Cuba's capital, you will become a true aficionado as you explore the attractions and absurdities, the historical riches and contemporary difficulties, of what was once known as "The Sugar Island."

"THE VIEW OF HAVANA WHEN ARRIVING INTO THE HARBOR IS ONE OF THE MOST PLEASANT AND PICTURESQUE SIGHTS ON THE COASTLINE OF THE AMERICAS NORTH OF THE EQUATOR."

Alexander von Humboldt

WALK

Fashion, Art & Architecture

A CULTURAL CATWALK THROUGH OLD HAVANA

Artistic landscapes, mythical places, and cult venues in Cuba's capital

The best way to stroll through Havana is in the footsteps of art. Our starting point is the Museo Nacional de Bellas Artes (National Museum of Fine Arts) **1**, founded in 1896, whose more than 47,000 objects make it one of the most important art collections in the Caribbean. The older section is in a palace-like structure built in 1927 on Plaza Central, with an entrance directly across from the Kempinski Hotel **2** and not far from Havana's defining structure, **El Capitolio 3**. The museum is a prime example of the eclectic architecture prevalent in Cuba, and it once housed the Asturian Club, which is

The signature building of Havana today is El Capitolio, built in 1929 and inspired by the Washington Capitol, the Panthéon in Paris, and St. Peter's Basilica in the Vatican. The Cuban National Assembly gathers here twice a year

now just minutes away at Boulevard Prado 309 and has restaurants and exhibition spaces. Just as the museum's facade mixes a wide variety of stylistic eras and building materials, so too the permanent exhibition combines different magnificent interiors: in addition to Egyptian sarcophagi and 3,500-year-old showpieces from Mesopotamia, there are examples of colonial art from both North and South America, as well as a patchwork of pieces from the Italian Renaissance, the Spanish Baroque period, eighteenth-century British painting, and nineteenth-century French painting, as well as a huge porcelain collection. But beware: not all the exhibits are original! In 1919, for example, the museum acquired seventy copies of famous paintings from Madrid's Prado.

Two blocks away, the Palacio de Bellas Artes (Palace of Fine Arts) **4**, designed by Alfonso Rodríguez Pichardo and opened in 1954, is the premier museum for Cuban art. The entrance is on Calle Trocadero, under an expressionist sculpture by Mateo Torriente Bécquer (1910–1966). Across the street

Wifredo Lam, *Le Mariage*, 1942, tempera on paper mounted on canvas, 192 × 124 cm

is the park of the Museo de la Revolución **5**, which features various improvised instruments of war used by the Cuban revolutionaries to rout Fulgencio Batista and his troops in 1959. In the Palacio one encounters—on 7,600 square meters and spread over three floors—key figures of Cuban art from the seventeenth century to the present. A highlight of the collection, which includes approximately 17,000 pieces, is the work of Wifredo Lam (1902–1982), a friend of Picasso and André Breton. His paintings, influenced by Cubism and Surrealism, hang today in New York's Museum of Modern Art and Guggenheim Museum. Lam's work is credited with rehabilitating the Afro-Cuban

Roberto Fabelo, *Tuerca* (Lug Nut), 2011, oil on canvas, 164 × 122 cm

Alfredo Sosabravo, *Dama del Sombrero* (Lady with a Hat), 2003, oil on canvas, 190 × 126 cm

heritage suppressed by the white elites and has served as a key inspiration for artists throughout Latin America.

After the 1959 revolution, the younger generation of Cuban artists who came after Wifredo Lam continued to be guided by the Western avant-garde, even though freedom to travel became heavily restricted. In the **National Museum 1**, one sees only isolated works of Socialist Realism, which was never transformed into a dogmatic formula in Cuba—unlike in Eastern Europe and the Soviet Union. Asked about her personal top ten in the collection, chief curator Margarita Gonzalez names these artists: Raúl Martínez (1927–1995), Antonia Eiriz (1929–1995), Ever Fonseca (b. 1938), Nelson Domínguez (b. 1947), Manuel Mendive (b. 1944), Aldo Menéndez (1948–2020), Roberto Fabelo (b. 1951), Zaida del Río (b. 1954), José Bedia (b. 1959), and Belkis Ayón (1976–1999). Only a few early paintings by Tomás Sánchez (b. 1948) hang in the National Museum of Fine Arts, as his works have long been unattainable for the museum, given Cuba's diminished cultural budget.

English-language tours of the National Museum, tailored especially for collectors and art enthusiasts, are offered by the **Máxima Estudio-Galería 6**,

Havana Cathedral (Catedral de San Cristóbal) where Pope John Paul II held a service in January 1998, as did Pope Francis in September 2015

located just across the street. There you can also see the portfolios of forty Cuban painters and photographers, represented with enormous passion and dedication by gallery owner Yaiset Ramírez. In addition to Roberto Fabelo, there are other internationally known figures such as Juan Suárez Blanco (b. 1953), Santiago Rodríguez Olazábal (b. 1955), René Peña (b. 1957), Moisés Finalé (b. 1957), Carlos Quintana (b. 1966), and Sandra Ramos (b. 1969).

After such a feast for the eyes, you may wish to engage your other senses, in which case take a stroll through the neighboring Calle Empedrado—and simply follow the swelling salsa music. At number 411 is Havana's best-known dance school, **La Casona del Son 7**, which transmits into the street a wide variety of Cuban rhythms. The twenty-five teachers here will lead you through a comprehensive repertoire of Cuban dance styles—and, since the pandemic, they also teach online! Silvia Canal's team welcomes everyone, whether you're a beginner or advanced, coming for a trial lesson or a two-week course with accommodation.

Continuing on Calle Empedrado in the direction of the harbor, you soon come across the **Havana Cathedral (Catedral de San Cristóbal) 8** (see also pp. 57–58). A few meters further along is La Bodeguita del Medio 9, one of Ernest Hemingway's many beloved bars during his twenty-one-year stay on the Sugar Island. Hemingway made the Bodeguita as famous for its mojitos as was the **El Floridita** ⑩ bar for its daiquiris. For decades, guests were allowed to sign the walls of the state restaurant as if it were a guest book. Sadly, during the pandemic, the management felt they had to repaint the walls, and autographs from all over the world, including those of many artists and writers, were simply whitewashed over. For those interested in following in Hemingway's traces further, head two street corners over to the **Hotel Ambos Mundos** ⑪. It was here that the passionate deep-sea fisherman stayed in the 1930s and completed his novel *For Whom the Bell Tolls*. His hotel room on the fifth floor can be visited today.

Across the street from the Bodeguita, one looks into the courtyard of the **Centro Wifredo Lam (Wifredo Lam Center for Contemporary Art)** ⑫, which is lined with murals by Austrian artist Clemens Krauss (b. 1981). The two-story eighteenth-century city palace is a hotspot for contemporary art and since 1984 has been the headquarters for the Havana Biennial, the first art biennale of the Global South. Unfortunately, financial constraints and political censorship have regularly caused this vital art event to be postponed or canceled, and in 2022 the fourteenth Havana Biennial was boycotted by the international art establishment in protest against the Cuban government's imprisonment of demonstrators and art activists.

Parallel to Calle Empedrado, at the end of the restaurant-lined street, is **Taller Experimental de Gráfica** ⑬, Havana's most famous graphics workshop. In 1962, muralist Orlando Suarez, with personal support from Che Guevara, founded the Taller Experimental de Gráfica together with ten other artist colleagues. Those who successfully make their way past the restaurants and their assertive maître d's armed with menus can watch graphic artists at work on museum-quality printing presses in a former warehouse, which the community printshop moved into in 1990. The graphics workshop is available free of charge to its more than one hundred registered members, which also have their own gallery for displaying and selling their freshly printed works. The director, Yamilys Brito, who is well connected in the international art scene, is regularly on site and happy to provide information about the work of her members.

On the way to the next art exhibition, you can enjoy delicious cocktails and tapas on the rooftop terrace of the restaurant **El Del Frente** ⑭, located at Calle O'Reilly 303. From there you can look out over the remarkable three-story structure of the art gallery **Factoría Habana** ⑮ across the street, commissioned by the Office of the City Historian and realized by architect

Abel San Miguel. Since 2010, Spanish-born founding director Concha Fontenla has provided the Cuban art scene with unique exhibition and experimental spaces there. But take note when asking around in the old town: most tourists are directed instead to the nearby brewery La Factoría 16 on the beautiful **Plaza Vieja 17**. Next to Fabelo's sculpture of a naked, rooster-riding warrior, and surrounded by live music, Cubans and tourists alike enjoy the products of Austrian brewing technology. Alternatively, Café El Escorial 18 across the street serves fresh-roasted coffee. Some of the colorful eighteenth- and nineteenth-century casitas that surround the plaza

Cohiba Lanceros—once the favorite cigar of Fidel Castro

are devoted entirely to contemporary art: Fototeca de Cuba 19, run by Lisette Ríos, behind a baby-blue facade; the Vitrina de Valonia 20 for Graphic Novels and Comic Culture; and the Centro de Desarollo de Artes Visuales 21 on the corner of San Ignacio, which organizes two important art salons every year. The **Plaza Vieja 17**, a former parade ground and later marketplace, offers even more curiosities for tourists, such as Cuba's impressive astronomic observatory Planetario 22 and, right next to it on the terrace of a corner building thirty-five feet high, the **Cámara Oscura 23** offering magnificent views over the entire old town. An absolute must!

Those who feel an urge to explore should walk down Calle Muralla toward the harbor. At the end of the street, opposite Havana's most elegant cigar store, **Cuervo & Sobrinos 24**, is Casa Museo Alejandro de Humboldt 25, dedicated to the polymath explorer and writer Alexander von Humboldt (1769–1859). Cubans still respectfully refer to the German—who visited their island twice, surveying and inventorying its flora and fauna—as "Cuba's second discoverer." The young director Juan Carlos Christy likes to guide visitors himself through the museum's permanent exhibition, donated by the German government. On leaving the Casa Museo Humboldt, a park opposite with a bust of the explorer invites visitors to linger.

Calle Oficios, which runs parallel to the harbor, lures visitors with its multiple sites of contemporary art production: at the intersection with Calle Luz, number 402e houses **Loft Habana** 26, with luxurious rooms for rent as well as an art gallery featuring multiple exhibitions throughout the year (see also p. 61). If you are interested in buying artwork, don't hesitate to contact Julia Leon, the gallery's friendly manager. And make sure to visit the rooftop terrace, where—in addition to Cuban cocktails and other local specialties—a breathtaking view over the harbor basin awaits. A hundred meters away at number 307b is the small **ONA Galería** 27, which serves as a launching pad for young artists. Lovers of design are advised to explore the side street Santa Clara. In number 8, the **Factoría Diseño** 28 invites you to visit its two floors. The Festival Diseño has taken place here since summer 2022, organized for the avant-garde of Cuban fashion and furniture design.

The **Galería Los Oficios** 29 at Calle Oficios 200 is devoted exclusively to the paintings and sculptural work of National Award–winner Nelson Domínguez (b. 1947 in Santiago de Cuba). With his expressionistic style, Domínguez became a leading figure of the so-called "Seventies Generation."

Halfway between, in the cross street Obrapía 108c, you can visit the body-art workshop **La Marca** 30, named the hippest art spot in Old Havana by Tripadvisor in 2023. Founder Leo Canosa opened Cuba's first professional tattoo studio here in 2015, and since then it's morphed into a cosmopolitan center for body and street art, while also offering dance and theater performances. The fact that La Marca's extremely diverse team is particularly concerned with working with young people from the district has been demonstrated by exhibitions such as *The Martyrs of Asphalt*, with artistically painted and decorated skateboards.

If you're in search of a jewelry gift or souvenir, stop three blocks away at Calle Cuba 467a at **Jorge Gil's jewelry store** 31, which also serves as a workshop. What's so special about his distinctive accessories is that they're made exclusively of titanium. This lightweight and consistently shiny metal, with an extremely high melting point of 1,666 degrees Celcius, is costly to produce, and anywhere else besides Cuba it would be virtually unaffordable for the average shopper.

The addresses of sustainable fashion labels are widely scattered across Old Havana. Between Plaza Vieja and the port, on the second floor of Calle San Ignacio 657, is **Beyond Roots** 32, Cuba's most en vogue boutique for Afro-Cuban fashion. Its founder, Adriana Heredia Sánchez, is a fashion

Collection by Beyond Roots with paper dress

pioneer who both outfits Havana's black hip-hop scene and offers Afro-Cuban women seminars on hair design and organic body care. For those interested in the Afro-Cuban religion of Santería, Adriana's team also organizes day trips to workshops in Havana's suburbs—sometimes a harsh contrast to the restored facades of the historic center!

The first Afro fashion brand in Cuba, BarbarA's Power 33, was founded in 2012 by Deyni Abreu Terry, a Black activist and lawyer who named it after her mother. The following year, she founded Alianza Unidad Real, which works to combat all manner of discrimination faced by Black Cubans. She runs a boutique at Calle Cienfuegos 211 together with the designer Yurena Manfugás, who has also put together a collection for children. BarbarA's Power is also a social project and has a children's club that aims to empower even the youngest Cubans.

Nearby in the courtyard of Calle Cuba 815 you'll find the **Rafael Trejo Boxing Gym** 34, offering foreign guests customized courses with real professionals. Boxing is the second most popular sport on the island after baseball, and some 20,000 Cubans are said to be organized in clubs. A stone's throw away at Calle San Isidro 214 is the art workshop and gallery Galería Taller Gorría 35. The name is derived from Jorge Perugorría, probably Cuba's best-known actor, who became world-famous with the film *Fresa y Chocolate* (*Strawberry & Chocolate*, 1993) and was allowed to rent this exemplary renovated building thanks to his good relations with the city historian. In addition to exhibitions and artist happenings, there are excellent concerts every week on the rooftop. From its two-story bar, you can look over the entire old town all the way to the landmark building El Capitolio. Not only are the city's best musicians regular guests here, but novelist Leonardo Padura, a friend of Jorge's, may also be found reading from his latest book. The once notorious waterfront is now known for its street art and artist activists. A stroll along the streets of

San Isidro, Merced, Acosta, and Picota 36 will lead you to impressive graffiti and murals.

But back to the busy center around the Plaza del Christo: opposite the **Iglesia del Santo Cristo (Christ Church)** 37, built in 1732 and a former place of pilgrimage for sailors, is Cuba's first store devoted to lingerie. Christiane Krämer from Germany founded her brand **Cris-Cris** 38 in Berlin in 2000 and fell in love with Cuba a little later. In addition to seductive lingerie, she now also offers imaginative swimwear at affordable prices. In her window displays, Krämer, a trained stage designer, likes to give her models a theatrical flair.

Just a minute from Cris-Cris, you'll find **Clandestina** 39. This trendy brand is a pioneer in textile recycling in Cuba and is known as an organizer of hip events even in Florida, where it has an offshoot. With their pithy slogans on T-shirts, bags, and other accessories, Idiana del Rio and Leire Fernandez have touched a nerve with Cubans—and sometimes get on their nerves. Their store is located at Calle San Ignacio 657, and they also sell goods online.

Just three blocks away, at Calle Amargura 253, you will find the three-person design collective **Dador** 40, which also has a branch in New York. The collections of Lauren Fajardo, Ilse Antón, and Raquel Janero differ from each other only in their varieties of beauty and can be worn at different times of the day. What unites them is their ethical and ecological approach. Loypa Izaguirre follows the same approach with her upbeat and floral summer fashion made from locally produced fabrics. Her

Collection by Cris-Cris in the Museo de Artes Decorativas

The Malecón with the Hotel Nacional, seen from the restaurant La Torre

brand **Color Café** **41** has a boutique at Calle Aguiar 109, which also includes a café where you can enjoy fresh Cuban coffee, cocktails, and tapas.

Must See Spots outside Old Havana

Those who wish to explore beyond Old Havana and venture into the western neighborhoods of Vedado and Miramar can do so in two ways: through the narrow and noisy alleys of Centro Habana or along the nine-kilometer-long waterfront promenade, the **Malecón** **42**. For classic car fans, the colorful convertible oldtimers called *almendrones*, whose bodies are mostly Buicks, Dodges, Plymouths, or Chevrolets from the '40s and '50s, are a good choice. For those who have already breathed in enough exhaust fumes, the **Museo del Automóvil** known as **El Garaje (The Garage)** **43** offers an exceptional collection of classic cars as well as three "Popemobiles" and the blue VW Beetle of world-famous author Alejo Carpentier. During the '40s and '50s, Cuba had the highest density of cars in all of Latin America. If you prefer a cheaper option, you should beckon one of the yellow Coco Taxis. These three-wheeled, eggshell-like vehicles are best suited for the narrow streets of Centro Habana, Cuba's most densely populated neighborhood. For those on foot, however, we recommend a stop at **Malecón 663** **44**, a boutique hotel run by Sarah Exposito. With two bars and four individually designed apartments named after well-known Cuban songs, this is a haven of Cuban art and music. The rooftop terrace beckons with its nightly concerts, delicious cocktails and snacks, and unforgettable views over Havana Bay. On Calle San Lazaro, which runs parallel to the waterfront, Laila Chaaban runs her zero-waste collection **Capicúa** **45** at number 55. The brand premiered during the thirteenth Havana Biennial in 2019 and has continued to captivate people with its elegance and colorful Afrotropicalisms.

Centro Habana also has a Chinatown, though one hardly encounters people from China anymore. Most of the Chinese who immigrated to Cuba in the early twentieth century paired up with Cuban partners, giving Cuba's cosmopolitan population another interesting dimension. A notable exponent of this history is the Anacaona, the first Cuban-Chinese women's jazz band, which was founded in 1932 by five sisters and celebrated its eighty-fifth anniversary in 2017. In a former cinema of the "barrio chino," at Calle Rayo 108, is the **Galleria Continua** **46**, originally based in the Italian town of San Gimignano and now with branches in Paris, Beijing, Rome, São Paulo, and Dubai. The names of the more than sixty Cuban artists it represents read like a who's who of the contemporary art scene. If you keep to the left when leaving the Galería, you'll soon come across numerous Chinese restaurants and martial art clubs, whose walls of pictures tell the story of this curious neighborhood.

On Calle Concordia there are several small private restaurants, called *paladares* in Cuba, to be recommended: for example, the eponymous **La Concordia** **47** or **La Guarida** **48**, which have airy dining terraces. On the corner of Calle Escobar, you can dine sumptuously in the historic **Michifú** **49**, and those who love baroque interiors mustn't miss **San Cristóbal Paladar** **50**, located at Calle San Rafael 469: the restaurant is crammed to the ceiling with memorabilia, and Barack Obama dined there when he visited Cuba in 2016, the first

The gourmet restaurant San Cristóbal Paladar has attracted notable figures such as Beyoncé, Jay-Z, and President Obama

state visit by a US president in eighty-eight years!

In socialist Cuba, private art galleries continue to be banned and—without protection "from above"—still have to disguise themselves as artists' studios, workshops, and apartments. The first apartment gallery was founded by curator Cristina Vives with photographer Antonio Figueroa in October 1995 at John Lennon Park in Vedado, Estudio Figeroa-Vives 51 . There they

The Chorrera Tower is now home to a beer garden and disco

still receive their now international clientele, including the Kennedy family. Their illustrious program includes stars such Alberto Korda, famous for his photo of Che Guevara, and Belkis Ayon, as well as a dozen young talents such as thirty-one-year-old Milton Raggi. For those who get a bit peckish after looking at pictures, there's the very atmospheric roof terrace of the restaurant Unión Francesa de Cuba 52 just 50 yards away. Diagonally across from there—in the basement!—is the happening rock club Submarino Amarillo (Yellow Submarine) 53 . About a dozen other galleries and several fashion studios are hidden in Vedado and the western neighborhoods of Miramar and Playa (an annotated list is in the appendix).

At the end of the Malecón promenade, by the delta of the Almendares River, appears the **Chorrera Tower** 54 . Built in order to defend Spanish settlers in the sixteenth century, today it attracts visitors with its restaurant terrace and disco. Next to the tower is the restaurant 1830 55 , located in a colonial villa and less known for its menu than for the salsa parties that take place in its Japanese-style garden. A little upriver, nature lovers will enjoy discovering the last piece of untouched jungle still in Havana, and in the bend of the Almendares two top-notch fish restaurants sit opposite each other. The rather simple Amigos del Mar 56 as well as Riomar 57 , in which President Obama once enjoyed a lobster masterpiece. The sommelier who served Obama that night later opened his own restaurant, Costa Vino 58 , located at the point where the Malecón disappears into a tunnel in order to reach

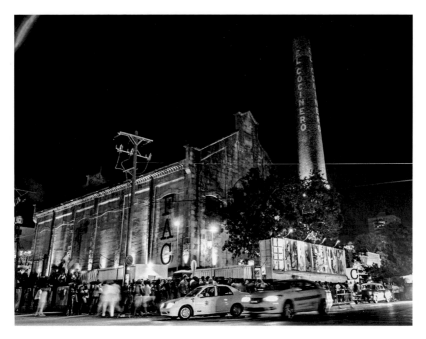

The Fábrica de Arte Cubano is a major venue for cinema, concerts, art, dance, and theater

the opposite bank of the river, reemerging as Fifth Avenue in the embassy district, Miramar.

Follow the riverside road on the left to arrive a few minutes later at Havana's hippest cultural institution: the **Fábrica de Arte Cubano** 59. This converted cooking-oil factory reopened its doors in 2014 and was named one of the world's most interesting cultural venues by *Time* magazine. Based on a concept by rock musician X Alfonso, founder of the legendary ethno-fusion band Síntesis, the culture factory has a three-story exhibition space, several bars and boutiques, restaurants, and stages, each of which hosts concerts, fashion shows and performances, and dance and theater shows from Thursday afternoon to Sunday night. The Fábrica is exemplary in many respects: as a place of international encounters, interdisciplinary art production, and economic entrepreneurship; apart from the employed curators, everyone here works on a volunteer basis. A personal recommendation: the restaurant El Cocinero 60, located just to the right of the Fábrica's main entrance. **MT**

FASHION

"WE'VE BEEN RECYCLING HERE SINCE COLUMBUS"

A short history of upcycling in Cuba

Upcycling has a long tradition in Cuba. Indeed, it was already in practice during the colonial period, when it was completely normal to pass on, adapt, and reuse clothing. For example, house slaves regularly received the worn-out clothes of their masters, which they accessorized with belts, lace, and colorful accessories, donning these garments on festive occasions. Such scenes were

The famous salsa singer Celia Cruz (1925–2003) in a Cuban bata dress, which mixes the influences of rumba, flamenco, and Caribbean carnival, ca. 1950

captured by the French painter Victor Patricio de Landaluze in his paintings of everyday life in Havana, depicting elegant Creole women and dressed-up gallants. The colorful and frilly bata dress, meant to imitate the wardrobe of wealthy European women and nowadays ubiquitous at folk festivals, is a perfect example of this, as it shows the intersection of African, French, and Spanish influences, as well as Caribbean carnival, rumba, and flamenco.

The harsh living conditions on the island, which originally had no industry of its own, forced people to be inventive. The bourgeoisie in the cities followed the trends of fashion centers abroad, and in the nineteenth century they looked mainly to Paris. After that, North

American influence prevailed, thanks mainly to Hollywood. In the 1950s, movie stars such as Errol Flynn, María Félix, and Maurice Chevalier bought their handmade clothes at the Cuban department store chain El Encanto. At that time, Havana was a fashion mecca for South and North America alike. Cubans with low incomes were also inspired by El Encanto's window displays and later had seamstresses reproduce the patterns—using fabrics from the wholesale market on Calle Muralla.

Another practice—a kind of emotional and generational contract—has survived to the present day: in Cuba, it was and still is customary to pass down pieces of clothing in one's family, adapting them according to the needs and fashions of the moment. Many such family heirlooms are reworked in unique ways while still bearing witness to the high emotional value they hold for their wearers. This tradition is followed by many designers in Cuba today, following the principle of selective and circular reuse and recycling of high-quality materials and fabrics. A circular economy on a small scale, in other words, as is done by the thirteen designers in the joint project HavanaTrapo. Although they each have an individual style, the fashion designers at HavanaTrapo share a common goal: to reduce environmentally harmful byproducts while creating one-of-a-kind pieces of high and long-lasting quality.

Upcycling is an environmentally friendly alternative to the current "buy, wear, and throw away" consumption model, and it will play a crucial role in a future circular economy, allowing consumers to customize their fashion tastes in a sustainable way. It's interesting to note how the fashion industry is now also using upcycling as an aesthetic for their seasonal trends. For example, in new collections that imitate retro and second-hand fashion, the potential of patchwork techniques is clearly evident. Meanwhile, even large department stores are using old clothes, mixing them with new fabrics. Upcycling therefore isn't just recycling, it's an ethical approach to our limited natural resources. **BPV & AVM**

➤ Some results from Josephine Barbe's upcycling workshop HabanaTrapo, showing a wide range of variations and individual styles through the reuse of second-hand clothes

Countless patios offer cool and relaxing oases in the otherwise bustling city. The model Jordan wears a hoodie influenced by the style of *tropicalismo* from the collection of Alain Marzán

◄ The shopping strip Calle
Obispo with a view of El Capitolio

Creations by the designers Camila Aguilar
and Alain Marzán from recycled denim

⌃ Plaza Vieja with the house of Conde de Cañongo, where today the Walloon Cultural Center is located

◂ The model Cesia in a design by Urpi Rincón

The designer Alain Marzán models his own recycled cotton fabrics

At Plaza Vieja, the model Lisandra
in front of a sculpture by the artist
Roberto Fabelo with an embroidered
denim Jacket from Camila Aguilera's
collection Kon To'

➤ The model Dagmar in an
outfit by Camila Aguilera

The fashion icon Gysleda de la
Barca in a dress with combined
crochet patterns on fine and
coarse fabrics by Monica García

➤ The models Wilma
and Deniye in everyday
clothing with patterns
by Aslin Asencio

37

Creations by Dora Jorrín in the tropical courtyard
of Loft Habana (see p. 61). The model Wilma (left)
with a summery frill top from green tulle and
palazzo pants with African wax prints. The model
Deniye (right) in evening dress with a fleece jacket
and tulle dress with floral printed hem and top

Daniela Hernández invents
new patterns from different
reassembled textiles

Summer fashion by Madelaine
Muñoa—including material from
recycled curtain fabrics—in front
of the former Governor's Palace
at the Plaza de Armas

> The model Cesia in front of the bust of the national poet Cirilio Villaverde (1812–1894), Plaza del Ángel

The models Thalía, Cesia, Nayelis, and Lisandra on the Plaza del Ángel with creations by Claudia Arcía and Boris Pérez

Unique upcycling pieces by Nilse
Fonseca and Ariadna Doeste on
the roof of the Palacio de Segundo
Cabo, Plaza de Armas

◄ Matching outfit from the collection Afro-Elegancia by Deborah Vázquez. Vázquez paints over a wide variety of garments, assembling them into a harmonious gallery of images that create a recognizable fashion line

Creations using the traditional patchwork technique *sashiko* for shirts and pants by Claudia Arcía and Boris Pérez in a bar of the Callejón de los Peluqueros (Barber's Alley)

"THE COUNTRY NEEDS NEW MATERIALS"

Cuba's potential for an innovative and sustainable textile industry

According to estimates by the European Commission, around six million tons of textiles are destroyed every year in Europe alone, including factory-fresh, unsold collections of so-called "fast fashion." Yet fashionable and sustainable clothing need not be a contradiction in terms. On the contrary, new organic fabrics offer unimagined prospects, especially for the countries of the Global South.

The conventional textile industry is one of the world's biggest polluters and is responsible for a significant proportion of global CO_2 emissions. Conventional cotton production in particular consumes enormous amounts of water and energy while polluting the soil with herbicides, pesticides, and even genetic engineering. To produce only one kilogram of cotton, up to 11,000 liters of water are needed. In addition, people in the cotton fields of the Global South usually work under unhealthy and inhumane conditions in order to keep prices down in the North. High time, therefore, to give alternative sustainable raw materials a chance.

Because Cuba doesn't grow cotton, doesn't have a textile industry worth mentioning, and is forced to import clothing—mostly cheap, synthetic, "Made in China" products—there is both a need and a great potential to develop alternative materials. Promising new directions

Josephine Barbe with a patchwork dress by Boris Pérez

▲ Hemp stem and hemp fibers on a hemp jersey

➤ Gysleda de la Barca with a top made of jersey with algae (Seacell)

include, for example, using hemp, bamboo, and algae, which find ideal growing conditions in Cuba and could help reduce dependence on imports.

Hemp is a real wonder plant in the textile market and has been used to make textiles for more than a thousand years. Hemp is hardy, grows quickly, and, unlike cotton, can be grown without pesticides. Hemp also requires much less arable land and water because, when the first hemp leaflet grows out of the earth, the roots have already reached the groundwater. The usable hemp fiber is located inside the plant, which can grow up to four and a half meters high, and clings to a lightweight wooden pole. During processing, the natural glue is washed out and the fiber is cottonized with enzymes. Textile hemp is then soft, durable, and antibacterial, and it can replace cotton in a variety of textiles, such as shirts, jeans, dresses, and hoodies.

Giant bamboo (*Dendrocalamus giganteus*)—an alternative to conventional cotton?

Bamboo is one of the fastest growing plants on earth, adaptive to different climates, resistant to pests, and requiring neither fertilizers nor pesticides. To create a textile fiber from bamboo, the lignified bamboo canes are ground and dissolved with a biodegradable substance to form a viscous spinning mass. After the solvent is washed out, the cellulose fiber regains its original properties, becoming very similar to cotton. This material, called lyocell, produces no contaminated wastewater.

To give the bamboo fiber an additional breathable function in sustainable sports textiles, purified and powdered brown algae could be added to the spinning solution to replace synthetic fibers such as polyester and polyamide. After all, in addition to CO_2-intensive polymer production and disposal, the fossil resource petroleum is finite and pollutes the environment through the abrasion of microplastics.

Regenerative algae are a fast-growing raw material from the sea that removes CO_2 from the atmosphere through photosynthesis. Algae manage without synthetic fertilizers and even benefit from global warming, which accelerates their growth. In the Caribbean in particular, Sargassum algae blooms have increased dramatically, flooding beaches by the ton. But what's a plague today could turn out to be a blessing tomorrow: dried, pulverized, and with a bamboo-algae admixture, the textiles produced from it feel silky soft on the skin, are durable, and can even be composted. So for Cuba and the entire Caribbean, it's an ideal sustainable fiber! **JB**

⌃ Removal of algae on the beach near Havana

❯ Brown algae, now a plague, tomorrow a new hope for the Caribbean?

⌄ Algae in powder form, as fiber, and as fabric (Seacell)

ARCHITECTURE

HAVANA: THE POLYCENTRIC CITY

Through the streets and squares of Old Havana back to the founding era of the Cuban capital

Originally named San Cristóbal de la Habana after Christopher Columbus, the capital of Cuba is the westernmost of seven cities founded by the Spanish conquistadors in the sixteenth century. With the official founding of Havana in 1519, the port was also moved to the bay of the same name. Its geostrategic location as a rallying point and transit port for the royal fleet—which had to

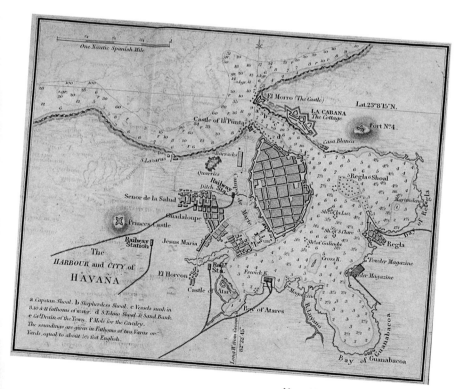

Map of Havana from the year 1882

The Plaza de Armas in the nineteenth century by Federico Mialhe, showing the former palaces of the governor and the fleet commander, now reopened as museums

make stops here on its way between the Spanish colonies of Latin America and the mother country—contributed significantly to Havana's rapid economic boom. The city's bourgeoisie owed their prosperity primarily to the countryside, which supplied the capital with a rich palette of livestock and plantation products: cured meat, tobacco, coffee, and above all sugar, which was Cuba's main export until the middle of the twentieth century.

Havana's growing importance is reflected in the granting of the city charter in 1592 and in the fortifications that surround the entire center, some of the most formidable of the Spanish colonial empire. The need to protect the most important port of the Spanish crown from external enemies shaped both social life and the architectural image of the city. The City Hall and other

administrative buildings, churches, and convents are fortress-like in the Hispanic-Arabic style typical of Havana's old town, whose traces we also find in the palaces and private houses of that neighborhood. Typical of the historic center is the *casa habanera* with its patio: an open courtyard surrounded on the second floor by a circular gallery with columns. This patio represented the main axis of all family and social life. In front of the gate-like entrance on the first floor, merchants and dockworkers, businessmen and administrators pursued their activities, which were determined by the rhythm of the incoming Spanish galleons, their loading and unloading at the docks.

The Plaza de Armes with the Castillo de la Real Fuerza—completed in 1577 by slaves and prisoners of war—formed the center of the once-burgeoning sugar metropolis and its port. The lush trees of the Plaza de Armas not only provide shade for passersby, but also shelter numerous species of birds.

The Plaza de la Catedral with its Cathedral San Cristóbal, inaugurated in 1777, is located above a former marshy area near the harbor entrance. In 1592, the city's first aqueduct was built here—the first ever in the Spanish colonial empire—to supply water to

Plaza de la Catedral by Federico Mialhe, 1840, showing the cathedral's facade made of shell limestone with its asymmetrical bell towers

local residents and ships in the harbor. The cathedral, planned by the Jesuits, could only be completed in 1777 after thirty years of construction. It's surrounded by former city palaces, which today house art galleries, restaurants, and museums such as the Museo de Arte Colonial (Museum of Colonial Art).

From this first and largest square of the old town, we follow the narrow streets Oficios and Mercaderes in a southeasterly direction, passing the Plaza San Francisco with its baroque Franciscan monastery to the spectacular Plaza Vieja. This former market and fairground has a surprising uniformity to its house facades and offers an even rhythm of balconies and galleries, colonnades and archways, leading back into the patios (inner courtyards) that are typical to Cuba.

Plaza Vieja, located in the center of the four oldest squares in Havana, painted by an unknown artist in the eighteenth century

To the west, Plaza Vieja leads across Calle Teniente Rey to Plaza del Cristo. This square was created in 1640, where a modest chapel of Christ once stood against the city walls. To this day, Plaza del Cristo has maintained its original character with its seafarers' church, cobbled streets, and benches shaded by trees.

Today, if we look at the old town in its extension and hierarchical gradations, it becomes clear how the public squares served as starting points for its development. They are connected to each other by straight street axes, which also include other public spaces and form the image of a polycentric city. **RGM**

CUBAN MODERNITY IN HISTORICAL GARB

Examples of architectural upcycling in Old Havana's historic buildings

In the 1980s, the Cuban government commissioned urban historian Leal Spengler to restore Old Havana, whose buildings were in a state of increasing decay. The Cuban government, in conjunction with the Office of the Historian of the City of Havana (OHC), forged a collaborative partnership with UNESCO. The repair and renovation work was also accompanied by educational programs designed to teach residents about the importance of cultural heritage and involve them in the process of rehabilitating the old town.

Today, Old Havana is a UNESCO World Heritage Site and a preeminent attraction for visitors from across the world. The revival of social and cultural life in the historic center has also paid off economically. In the course of the economic reforms of recent years, new companies have been founded and numerous jobs created, especially in the service sector. In the process, freelance teams of architects have found opportunity in those cases where cooperation between state-owned firms and the private sector reaches its limit. Despite ongoing shortages and the rise in price of building materials, a number of unusual architectural projects, in collaboration with local craftsmen and artists, have been realized in recent years. Each project represents a unique challenge for which individual concepts and technical solutions have to be found; therefore, when planning projects, it's essential to archive knowledge and incorporate innovative recycling. Here are some examples of the "soft" upcycling of Old Havana's historic building fabric. **SPR**

Loft Habana (2010)
*Hotel with ten lofts, an art gallery,
a restaurant and rooftop bar*

Planning: José Antonio Choy
Project team: Adriana Choy León,
Olivia Choy León, Raúl Cruz Espinosa,
Jorge Luís Sam, Alejandra Pino

Oficios 402, between Luz and Acosta,
Habana Vieja
info@estampacuba.com

Loft Havana is in a building originally constructed in 1890 for private residences. In 2010, it was renovated and converted into a guesthouse. After the victory of the Cuban Revolution, the high rooms of this former Spanish city palace were divided into apartments, from which the architects realized ten luxurious lofts of various layouts, distributed around a tropically landscaped inner courtyard. The hotel also serves as an art gallery and has a bar and restaurant on the rooftop terrace, offering an unforgettable view over the harbor.

Any interested buyers can feel free to contact the friendly manager, Julia Leon. A visit to the terrace is highly recommended!

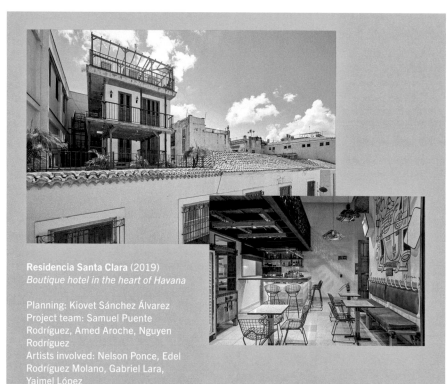

Residencia Santa Clara (2019)
Boutique hotel in the heart of Havana

Planning: Kiovet Sánchez Álvarez
Project team: Samuel Puente
Rodríguez, Amed Aroche, Nguyen
Rodríguez
Artists involved: Nelson Ponce, Edel
Rodríguez Molano, Gabriel Lara,
Yaimel López

Santa Clara 13, between Oficios and
Avenida del Puerto, Habana Vieja
info@residenciahotels.com

In 2014, the architectural firm Ad Urbis began the conversion of the Santa Clara Residence, a listed building. This corner structure is part of an ensemble of buildings from the nineteenth century. When it was converted into a four-story boutique hotel, the living space was expanded considerably, in part to create new common areas. By transforming the corridors, courtyards, and residential galleries into meeting places, a new residential landscape of private and communal spaces was created.

The furniture and wall decorations, the cast-iron railings and wood paneling were realized with neighborhood craftsmen and artists who recycled materials from the historic structure and gave them new functions.

Loft O'Reilly (2022)
Private vacation rental (Airbnb)

Architects: Islay Martínez, Sandra Becerra

Calle O'Reilly 512, apt. 1, between
Villegas and Avenida Bélgica, Habana Vieja

The sixty-square-meter Loft O'Reilly is located on the second floor of an art deco building on Calle O'Reilly. The building, which dates back to the first half of the twentieth century, features a magnificent facade and simple interiors. Architects Sandra Becerra and Islay Martínez decided to connect the spaces with two existing breezeways, expanding them into light and ventilated court-yards. In some places, the walls were stripped of plaster to allow the historicity and different construction eras of the building to stand out.

Bar Fajoma (2019)
Bar and restaurant

Planning: Kiovet Sánchez Álvarez + Hidden Fortress
Project team: Ana Laura Hernández Antuñas

Compostela 313, between Obispo and Obrapía, Habana Vieja
hola@fajoma.bar

This former residential building from the first half of the twentieth century was renovated and furnished in the style of the 1950s. Spread over the two-story mezzanine and the tropically planted roof terrace, there are now bars and restaurants with different offerings, a smoking salon, and two concert stages. In the Fajoma bar, you can find DJs and musicians from Cuba and abroad, of various approaches and styles, from jazz to hip-hop to drum and bass.

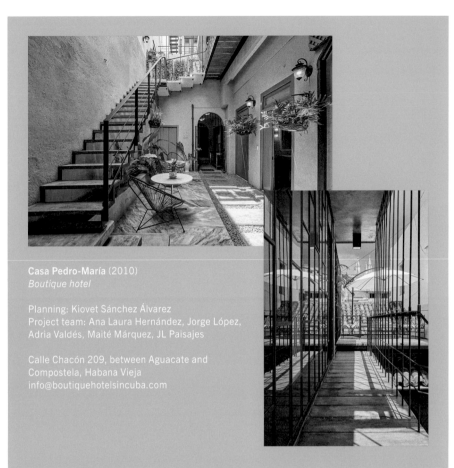

Casa Pedro-María (2010)
Boutique hotel

Planning: Kiovet Sánchez Álvarez
Project team: Ana Laura Hernández, Jorge López,
Adria Valdés, Maité Márquez, JL Paisajes

Calle Chacón 209, between Aguacate and
Compostela, Habana Vieja
info@boutiquehotelsincuba.com

Three-star hotel in the heart of the popular nightlife district Santo Angel, with six light-filled double rooms and suites connected by open staircases in the leafy open-air patio. The former nineteenth-century residence was given two additional floors with verandas and a shaded rooftop terrace with cocktail bar. Behind the colonial facade, open stone walls and wooden portals harmonize with glass and metal elements of contemporary architecture. Even the understated furnishings blend old and new with craftsmanship and art.

EVERYDAY UPCYCLING IN HAVANA

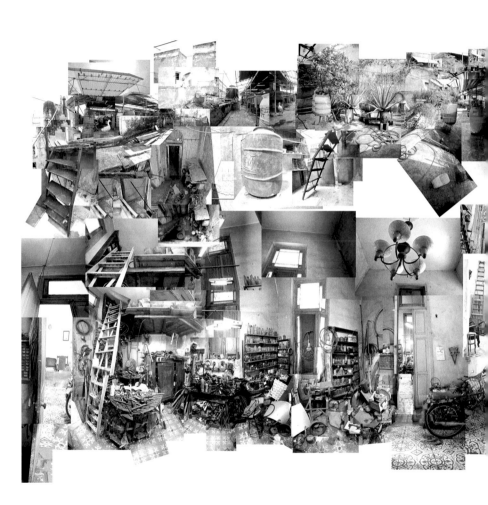

Nelson's Home (2012−23) by **Alfredo Ramos (Cuba) and Katarzyna Badach (Poland)**
In this collage the artists show the daily and widespread use of upcycling and recycling
in Cuban households (with rooftop gardens and poultry farming) as exemplified by Nelson,
a Cuban artist who lives and works in Havana

APPENDIX

USEFUL ADRESSES

We have used the @ symbol to point you to each online presence, without specifying the specific platform. The @ address may refer to a standard homepage, Tripadvisor listing, Facebook page, Instagram feed, etc. In Cuba, web pages may only exist for a short period, or are not reliable due to power outages and other disruptions. Therefore, a general @ address is provided, so that you can always be up to date.

Bars & Cafés

Café del Ángel *Most relaxing terrace in the old city*
Plaza del Ángel, Habana Vieja
@cafedelangeljf.com
+53 7 8644029

Café El Escorial 18 *Café and roastery*
Plaza Vieja, corner of Calle Muralla, Habana Vieja
@restaurantguru.com/Cafe-El-Escorial-Havana
+53 7 8683545

El Café *Fresh salads and fruit drinks*
Calle Amargura 358, Habana Vieja
@elcafehavana
+53 7 8613817

El del Frente 14 *Rooftop cocktail bar and restaurant*
Calle O'Reilly 303, Habana Vieja
@EldelFrente303
+53 7 8674256

El Floridita 10 *Daiquiri bar and restaurant frequented by Hemingway*
Calle Obispo 557, corner of Calle Monserrate, Habana Vieja
@barfloridita.com
+53 7 8671300

Fajoma Bar *Covering three floors and a rooftop*
Calle Compostela 313, Habana Vieja
+53 7 8621656

Jesús María *Rooftop bar and art gallery*
Calle Jesús María 20, Centro Habana
@RestauranteJesusMaria20
+53 5 4483296

King Bar *Music venue and dance hall*
Calle 23 N° 667, Vedado
@kingbarhavana
+53 7 8330556

La Bodeguita del Medio 9 *Mojito bar frequented by Hemingway*
Calle Empedrado 207, Habana Vieja
@labodeguitadelmedio.oficial
+53 7 8671374

La Factoría 16 *Popular open-air beer bar*
Plaza Vieja, Habana Vieja
+53 7 8664453

Madrigal Bar-Café *Artistic bar and café*
Calle 17 N° 809, Vedado
@Madrigal.Bar.Cafe
+53 7 8312433

Malecón 663 44 *Art hotel bar and music terrace*
Avenida Malecón 663, Centro Habana
@malecon663
+53 5 2735738
info@malecon663.com

Máximo Bar *Cocktail and tapas bar*
Calle Cuba 6, Habana Vieja
@maximobarOldHavana
+53 7 8015171

Sloppy Joe's Bar *Film location for "Our Man in Havana"*
Calle Zulueta 252, corner of Calle Agramonte, Centro Habana
@sloppyjoes.org
+53 7 8667157

Submarino Amarillo 53 *Much beloved by Cuban rock fans*
Calle 17, corner of Calle 6, Parque John Lennon, Vedado
@facebook.com/SubmarinoAmarilloOficial
+53 7 8320857

El Surtidor *Rooftop bar with a panoramic view*
Hotel Gran Manzana Kempinski, Habana Vieja
Calle San Rafael / Parque Central José Martí
@kempinski.com/en/
gran-hotel-kempinski-la-habana
+53 7 8699100

Terrazza Mirabana *Rooftop bar with music and a pool*
Hotel Parque Central Iberostar
Parque Central, Habana Vieja
@hotelparqcentral.com/apothecary-lounge
+53 7 8699100

Fashion Studios & Boutiques

BarbarA's Power (33)
Calle Cienfuegos 211, Habana Vieja
@barbaraspowercuba
+53 5 6849562

Beyond Roots (32)
Calle San Ignacio 657, Habana Vieja
@beyondroots.net
+53 7 8615072

Capicúa (45)
Calle San Lázaro 55, Habana Vieja
@capicua_fashion
+53 5 2845887

Clandestina (39)
Calle Villegas 403, corner of Teniente Rey,
Habana Vieja
@clandestina.co
+53 7 8600997

Color Café (41)
Calle Aguiar 109, Habana Vieja
@colorcafehabana.com
+53 5 2458903

Cris-Cris (38)
Plaza del Cristo, Habana Vieja
@criscris.cris.10
havanna.criscris@gmail.com

Dador (40)
Calle Amargura 253, Habana Vieja
@dadorhavana.com
+53 5 9733010

El Encanto (online only)
@elencantoatelier
+53 5 8416039

Habana Modas
Calle Aguila 453, Habana Vieja
@Habanamodas
+53 5 5515962

FENG (online only)
@nowinterisland.com/feng
+53 5 4312180

Innatus
Avenida del Puerto
Almacenes San José, 2nd floor, Habana Vieja
@innatus.cuba
+53 5 5578119

Salomé Modas
Calle 28, between Calle 1 and Calle 3, Miramar
@salomé-casa-de-modas
+53 7 2035070

Wasasa (online only)
@wasasa.eu
wasasa.eu@gmail.com
+43 6 9010193267

Galleries & Museums

Artista x Artista (AxA) *Foundation of the artist Carlos Caraicoa, with artist residency*
Calle 6 N° 702, apt. 2, corner of Avenida 7,
Miramar
@artistaXartista
+53 5 2055076

Casa Museo Alejandro de Humboldt (25) *With a permanent exhibition on the famous polymath*
Calle Oficios 254, Habana Vieja
+53 7 8012950
Tue–Sat, 9:30am–5:00pm

Centro de Desarollo de las Artes Visuales (21)
Plaza Vieja, Habana Vieja
+53 7 8018533
Mon–Sat, 10:00am–5:00pm

Centro Wifredo Lam (12) *Art space and headquarters of the Havana Biennale*
Calle San Ignacio 22, corner of Calle Empedrado,
Habana Vieja
@wlam.cult.cu
+53 7 8612096
Tue–Sun, 11:00am–4:00pm;
closed Sun and Mon

El Apartamento *Artist gallery on the top floor of an apartment building*
Calle 15 N° 313, apt. 3, corner of Calle H, Vedado
@artapartamento.com
+53 7 8356019
Tue–Sat, by appointment

Estudio Figueroa-Vives (51) *Artist apartment converted into a gallery*
Calle 21 N° 303, apt. 2, Parque John Lennon, Vedado
@EstudioFigueroaVives.com
+53 7 8326332

Factoría Habana (15) *Contemporary art in a historical space*
Calle O'Reilly 308, between Calle Habana and Calle Aguiar, Habana Vieja
@factoriahabana
+53 5 3589585
Mon–Sat, 9:00am–3:00pm; closed Sun

Factoría diseño (28) *Exhibition space and shop for Cuban design*
Santa Clara 8, between Calle Oficios and Avenida del Puerto, Habana Vieja
@factoria-design-habana
+53 5 5814268
Tue–Sat, 10:00am–5:00pm; closed Sun and Mon

Fototeca de Cuba (19) *National photo center with contemporary exhibitions*
Plaza Vieja, Habana Vieja
@fototecadecuba
+53 7 8018530
Tue–Sat, 10:00am–4:00pm

Galería ARTIS 718 *Contemporary art from Cuba presented with aesthetic sophistication*
Calle 7, corner of Calle 18, Miramar
@Galería-ARTIS-718
+53 7 204 7106

Galería Habana *State gallery with impressive artist archive*
Calle Línea 460 E, Vedado
@galeriahabana
+53 7 8327101 / 7 8314646

Galería La Acacia *State gallery founded in 1981 and located across from the Capitolio*
Calle San José 114, Centro Habana
@acaciagallery
+53 7 8613533 / 8639364

Galería La Nave *Hidden in a courtyard, curated by the master Jorge Peré*
Calle 18 N° 512, corner of Calle 5 and Calle 7, Miramar, Cuba
@lanave-galeria
+53 5 9968370

Galería Los Oficios (29)
Calle Oficios 166, Habana Vieja
@nelsondominguezart.com
+53 7 8630497

Galería Servando *A large number of interesting young artists*
Calle 23, corner of Calle 10, Vedado
@servandoartgallery
+53 7 8306150

Galería Taller Gorría (35) *Artist workshop, music venue, and restaurant with two rooftop terraces*
Calle San Isidro 214 E, Habana Vieja
@galeriatallergorria.com
+53 7 8646713

Galleria Continua (46) *Havana's most international gallery, located in an old cinema*
Calle Rayo 108, Barrio Chino, Centro Habana
@galleriacontinua.com/about/habana
+53 5 2542746 / 5 3411185

La Marca (30) *Body art studio, gallery, and social project*
Calle Obrapia 108C, Habana Vieja
@lamarcabodyart.com
+53 7 8012026

Máxima Galería (6) *Showing classics of Cuban modernism*
Calle Monserrate, corner of Calle Tejadillo, Habana Vieja
@maximagallerycuba
+53 7 2584217 / 7 8630205
Mon–Fri, 10:00am–6:00pm; Sat/Sun, 10:00am–5:00pm

Museo de Arte Colonial *Featuring colonial interiors from the eighteenth century*
Calle San Ignacio 61, Habana Vieja
@tripcuba.org/colonial-art-museum-havana
+53 7 8017458
Tue–Sun, 10:00am–6:00pm; Sun, 8:00am–12:00pm

Museo de la Revolución ⑤
Calle Refugio 1, Habana Vieja
@wikipedia.org/wiki/
Museum_of_the_Revolution_(Cuba)
Daily, 10:00am–5:00pm

Museo del Automóvil "El Garaje" ㊸ *Featuring the cars of revolutionaries and stars*
Calle San Ignacio 305-307-309, Habana Vieja
@museodelautomovilohch
+53 7 8018159
Tue–Sat, 9:30am–4:30pm;
Sun, 9:30am–1:00pm

Museo de Artes Decorativas *A little Versailles with 30,000 pieces on display*
Calle 17 N° 502, corner of Calle D, Vedado
@facebook.com/museodeartesdecorativas
+53 7 8320924
Wed–Mon, 10:00am–5:00pm

Museo Nacional de Bellas Artes ① *Universal arts: from Nubian sculpture to Dutch painting*
Calle San Rafael, between Calle Zulueta and Calle Monserrate, Habana Vieja

Museo Napoleónico *Featuring Napoleon's telescope and death mask*
Calle San Miguel 1, corner of Calle Ronda, Vedado
@napoleon.org/en/magazine/places/museo-napoleonico-cuba-2
+53 7 8791412
Tue–Sat, 9:30am–5:00pm;
Sun, 9:30am–12:30pm

Museo del Ron Havana Club *Museum tours with rum tasting*
Avenida del Puerto 262, corner of Calle Sol, Habana Vieja
@havanaclubmuseum.com/en/home
+53 7 8618051 / 7 8624108
Mon–Fri, 9:00am–4:30pm

ONA Galería ㉗ *Featuring emerging Cuban artists*
Calle Oficios 307b, Habana Vieja
@onagaleria.com
+53 7 8636338 / 5 9110268

Palacio de Bellas Artes ④ *Premier museum for Cuban art / World's largest collection of works by Wifredo Lam*
Calle Trocadero, between Calle Zulueta and Calle Monserrate, Habana Vieja
@bellasartes.co.cu
+ 53 7 8620140 / 7 8613858 / 7 8615757
Thu–Sat, 9:00am–5:00pm;
Sun, 10:00am–2:00pm

Palacio de los Capitanes Generales
City museum in the former governor's palace
Plaza de Armas, Habana Vieja
@wiki/Palacio_de_los_Capitanes_Generales
Daily, 10:00am–6:00pm

Palacio del Segundo Cabo *Museum of Caribbean Pirates and Cuban-European Relations*
Plaza de Armas, Habana Vieja
@wiki/Palacio_del_Segundo_Cabo
Daily, 10:00am–6:00pm

Planetario ㉒ *Interactive museum with themed rooms*
Plaza Vieja, corner of Calle Mercaderes, Habana Vieja
@planetariohabana
+53 7 8018544
Wed–Sat, 9:30am–6:00pm;
Sun, 10:00am–3:00pm

Taller Chullima *Studio of the artist Wilfredo Prieto in a boathouse on the Almendares River*
Calle 6 N° 905, between Calle 9 and Calle 11, Miramar
@tallerchullima
+53 7202 3654

Taller Experimental de Gráfica de La Habana ⑬
Graphic workshop with exhibitions
Callejón del Chorro, Habana Vieja
@TEGdeLaHabana
+53 7 8620979
Mon–Sat, 9:00am–3:00pm; closed Sun

Villa Manuela *Gallery of the union of artists and writers UNEAC*
Calle H 406, between Calle 17 and 19, Vedado
@galeriavillamanuela.com
+53 7 8322391
Mon–Fri, 10:00am–5:00pm

Vitrina de Valonia 20 *Cultural center for*
graphic novels
Plaza Vieja, Habana Vieja
@vitrinadevaloniahabana
+53 7 8697369
Mon—Fri, 9:30am—5:00pm

HOTELS & PENSIONS

ArteHotel *Featuring an artistic interior,*
owned by the movie star Laura de la Uz
Calle 2 N° 210, Vedado
@calle2.net
+53 7 8309079

Boutique Hotel Claxon *With rooftop terrace*
and top-quality restaurant Fangi
Calle Paseo 458, Vedado
@claxonhotel.com
+53 7 8322712 / 5 0956914

Casa Amistad *Right by El Capitolio, run by*
a German-Cuban couple
Calle Amistad 378, Habana Vieja
@casa-amistad.net
+53 5 2594108

Casa Boutique Viva la Vida *With a rooftop terrace*
and bike rentals
Calle 21 N° 507 A, Vedado
@vivalavidacuba.com
+53 7 8375017 / 5 3172247

Casa Pedro-María *With open-air patio and*
rooftop terrace
Calle Chacón 209, between Aguacate and
Compostela, Habana Vieja
@boutiquehotelsincuba.com
+53 7 8614641

Casa Santi *Pleasant family hotel in the*
historic center
Calle Cuarteles 120, Habana Vieja
@casa-santy-habana-vieja.maxicuba.com
+34 6 17391185

Hostal La Reserva *With an excellent garden*
restaurant
Calle 2 N° 508, Vedado
@lareservavedado.com
+53 7 8335244

Hotel Ambos Mundos 11 *Hemingway's room,*
number 511, can still be visited
Calle Obispo 151, Habana Vieja
@gaviotahotels.com/de/hotels-kuba/havanna/
hotel-ambos-mundos
+53 7 8609529

Hotel Gran Manzana Kempinski 2 *The best*
hotel on the Parque Central
Calle San Rafael / Parque Central José Martí,
Habana Vieja
@kempinski.com/en/gran-hotel-kempinski-
la-habana
+53 7 869 9100

Hotel Loma del Ángel *Nineteenth-century charm*
and modern design
Calle Cuarteles 104, Habana Vieja
@lomadelangel.com
+53 8015585 / 5 5388402

Hotel Nacional *Built by the mafia in 1930,*
with a charming park and view of the sea
Calle 21, corner of Calle O, Vedado
@hotelnacionaldecuba.com
+53 7 8363564

Hotel Parque Central Iberostar *Rooftop terrace*
with a bar and pool
Calle Prado, corner of Parque Central José Martí,
Habana Vieja
@ibercuba.com/br/hoteis/la-habana/
iberostar-parque-central
+34 871 620308

Hotel Telégrafo Axel *Meeting spot for the*
LGBTQ+ community
Calle Prado, corner of Parque Central José Martí,
Habana Vieja
@axelhotels.com/de/telegrafo-axel-hotel-la-
habana/hotel.html
+53 7 8610114

Loft Habana 26 *Ten exquisite design lofts with*
Cuban art
Calle Oficios 402 E, corner of Calle Luz, Habana
Vieja
@estampacollection.com/collection-houses/loft
+53 5 258 8540

Loft O'Reilly *A favorite of Airbnb customers*
Calle O'Reilly 512, Habana Vieja
@islay.matinezfernandez
+53 5 8269451

Residencia Santa Clara
Santa Clara 13, Habana Vieja
@residenciahotels.com
+53 7 8644858

Restaurants

Al Carbón *Cuban specialties with retro flair*
Calle Aquacate 9, corner of Calle Chacon,
Habana Vieja
@alcarbon.cuba
+53 7 8639697

Atelier *Havana's first paladar (private restaurant),
favored by artists*
Calle 5 N° 511, Vedado
@Restaurant-Atelier-Cuba
+53 7 8362025

Café Laurent *Excellent and chic, with terrace,
on the fifth floor of an apartment building*
Calle M N° 257, Vedado
@Paladar_Cafe_Laurent-Havana
+53 7 8312090

Costa Vino 58 *For gourmands and wine
enthusiasts*
Calle Calzada 1209, Vedado
@costavino.com
+53 5 2907255 / 5 2635813

El Cocinero 60 *Terrace restaurant next to the
Fabrica de Arte*
Calle 26, corner of Calle 11, Vedado
@elcocinerocuba.com
+53 7 8322355

Doña Alicia *Best rating on Tripadvisor*
Calle Reina 473, Chinatown, Centro Habana
@RestauranteDaAlicia
+53 7 8666009

Elizalde *Traditional food excellently prepared*
Calle Empedrado 521, Habana Vieja
@elizaldehabana
+53 5 3229650 / 7 8672157

Fangio *Star chef Sergio serves up Spanish
specialties*
In the Boutique Hotel Claxon, Avenida Paseo
458, Vedado
@fangiohabana.com
+53 7 8322712

Habana Mía *On the first floor, with view of the sea*
Calle Paseo 7, Vedado
@habanamia7
+53 7 8302287

Hecho en Casa *A new menu daily by chef Alina*
Calle 14 N° 511, Miramar
@hechoencasacuba.com
+53 7 2025392

Ivan Chef Justo *A charming vision of Havana
hidden on the first floor*
Calle Aguacate 9, corner of Calle Chacón,
Habana Vieja
@ivanchefsjusto
+53 7 8639697

La Concordia 47 *With rooftop terrace and clear
view over Centro Habana*
Calle Concordia 453, Centro Habana
@aconcordiarestaurant
+53 7 8644977

La Guarida 48 *With a film-ready interior and
generous terrace*
Calle Concordia 418, Centro Habana
@laguarida.com
+53 7 8669047

La Torre *Featuring a sky bar and breathtaking
view over Havana*
On the thirty-third floor of the Focsa building,
entrance at Calle 17, Vedado
@proyectoespacios.com/restaurante-la-torre/
+53 7 5533088

Los Mercaderes *Successful example of
Cuban-Italian fusion cuisine*
Calle Mercaderes 6, Habana Vieja
@paladarlosmercaderes
+53 7 8012437

Michifú 49 *Luxury culinary oasis with
Andalusian patio*
Calle Concordia, corner of Calle Escobar,
Centro Habana
@facebook.com/people/Michifú
+53 7 8624869

Otramanera *Excellent Catalonian-Caribbean
cuisine*
Calle 35 N° 1810, between Calle 20 and
Calle 41, Playa
@otramanera.lahabana
+53 7 2038315

San Cristóbal Paladar 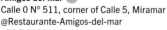 *High-class salon style with Havana relics and Santeria altar*
Calle San Rafael 469, Centro Habana
@san-cristobal-paladar-havana
+53 7 8601705

Tocamadera *Spanish specialties favored by diplomats*
Calle 38, between Calle 1 and Calle 3, Miramar
@tocamaderahabana
+53 5 2812144

Unión Francesa de Cuba *Founded in 1925, oldest French clubhouse in Cuba*
Calle 17, corner of Calle 6, Parque John Lennon, Vedado
@restaurantguru.com/Union-Francesca-Havana
+53 7 8324493

5 Sentidos *Cuban nouvelle cuisine, offering meat and vegetarian dishes*
Calle San Juan de Dios 67, between Calle Compostela and Calle Habana, Habana Vieja
@paladar5sentidos
+53 7 8648699 / 5 6802037

7 Dias *Offering a view of the sea*
End of Calle 14 at the Playita 16, Miramar
@Restaurante-7-Dias-Havana
+53 7 2096889

1830 *Food and dancing in a colonial atmosphere on the Almendares estuary*
Avenida Malecón, corner of Calle 20, Vedado
@1830-Jardines-Havana
+53 7 553090

Fish Restaurants

Amigos del Mar
Calle 0 N° 511, corner of Calle 5, Miramar
@Restaurante-Amigos-del-mar
+53 7 2031196

Nero di Sepia
Calle 6 N° 122, Miramar
@nerodiseppiacuba
+53 5 4787871

Riomar
Avenida 3 N° 11, La Puntilla, Miramar
@restauranteriomar
+53 7 2094838

Vegetarian and Vegan Cuisine

California
Calle 19, between Calle N and Calle O, Vedado
@californiacafehavana.com
+53 5 4630981

Camino al Sol
Avenida 3 N° 363, across from the Meliá Cohiba Hotel
@camino-al-sol-havana
+53 7 8321861

Ceperie Oasis Nelva
Calle Muralla, corner of Calle Habana, Habana Vieja
@oasisnelva
+53 5 2939758

El Shamuskiao
Calle Consulado 314, Centro Habana
@elshamuskiao
+53 5 2707346 / 7 8639150

ATTRACTIONS

Artecorte *Barack Obama had his hair done here by "Papito" Villadares*
Nonprofit organization that trains youth in hair styling
Callejón de los Peluqueros (Barber's Alley), Habana Vieja
@artecorte.org/en
+53 7 801 5102/5125

Bodegón21 *Secret grocery and snack bar*
Calle 21 N° 409 B, Vedado
@bodegon21
+53 5 1967882

Callejón de Hamel *Rumba concerts and street art*
Between Calle Aramburu and Calle Hospital
@atlasobscura.com/places/callejon-de-hamel
Concerts on Sat and Sun, starting at noon

Cámara Oscura *Offers a 360-degree view over Havana*
Plaza Vieja, corner of Calle Oficios, Habana Vieja
@camara-oscura-de-la-habana
+53 7 8664461

Centro Cultural Bertolt Brecht *Hotspot of contemporary theater, dance, and music*
Calle 13, corner of Calle I, Vedado
@centroculturalbertoltbrecht
+53 78329359

Centro Dulce María Loynaz *Villa of Cuba's best-known poet (1903–1997)*
Calle 19 N° 502, Vedado
@CentroLoynaz
+53 7 8320331
Mon–Fri, 10:00am–4:00pm

Chorrera Tower ⑤④ *Offering a beer garden and disco*
Westernmost cnd of the Malecón at the Almendares River between Vedado and Miramar

Cine Yara *Legendary Warner Brothers cinema from 1947 with 1,600 seats*
Corner of Calle 23 and Calle 0, Vedado
@cinematreasures.org/theaters/16889
+53 7 8329431

Coco Blue *Open-air nightclub with concert stage*
Calle 14 N° 112 E, Vedado
@coco-blue-la-zorra-pelua
+53 5 9121916
Concerts Thu–Sun starting at 9:00pm

Coppelia *Ice cream parlor of the socialist people with '60s concrete architecture*
Calle 23, corner of Calle L, Vedado
@wiki/Coppelia_(ice_cream_parlor)

Cuervo y Sobrinos ②④ *Café, Tobacco shop, and museum of chronometers*
Calle los Oficios, corner of Calle Muralla, Habana Vieja
@cuervoysobrinos.com
+53 7 8649515

El Capitolio ③ *Larger than the Capitol Building in Washington and seat of the Cuban parliament*
Calle Cienfuegos 66, Habana Vieja
@wiki/El_Capitolio
+53 7 8626536 / 7 8603411
Tue, Thu–Sat, 10:30am–4:00pm;
Wed and Sun, 10:30am–12:00pm

Fábrica de Arte Cubano (FAC) ⑤⑨ *Cultural center in a former factory*
Calle 26, corner of Calle 11, Vedado
@fac.cuba
+53 7 8382260
Thu–Sun, 6:00pm–2:00am

Gimnasio de Boxeo Rafael Trejo ③④ *Boxing classes with Cuban professionals*
Calle Cuba 815, Habana Vieja
@boxingcuba.blogspot.com
+53 7 8620266
Mon–Sat, 10:00am–6:30pm

Gran Teatro de la Habana "Alicio Alonso" *Home of the National Ballet of Cuba*
Parque Central José Martí, Habana Vieja
@wikipedia.org/wiki/Gran_Teatro_de_La_Habana
+53 7 8613077
Performances weekdays at 8:30pm and Sun at 5:00pm

Iglesia del Santo Cristo (Christ Church) ③⑦
Plaza del Cristo, Habana Vieja

Jardines de la Tropical *Unique Alhambra-style event location surrounded by tropical plants*
Hidden between Calle 41 and Avenida 46, Playa
@atlasobscura.com/places/
los-jardines-de-la-tropical
+53 7 8861767

Jorge Gil Estudio-Galería ③① *Handmade titanium jewelry*
Calle Cuba 467A, between Calle Amargura and Teniente Rey, Habana Vieja
@JorgeGilJewelry
+53 7 8018222 / 5 2724428

La Casa del Habano *Cigar shop with a large selection*
Avenida 5, corner of Calle 16, Miramar
@lacasadelhabano.com
+53 7 2144737

La Casona del Son ⑦ *Offering classes in all styles of Cuban dance*
Calle Empedrado 411, Habana Vieja
@lacasonadelson.com
+53 7 8616179
Mon–Sat, 9:00am–7:00pm; closed Sun

La Catedral de San Cristóbal de La Habana ⑧
Seat of the Archbishop, inaugurated in 1777
Plaza de la Catedral, Habana Vieja
Mass at 6:00pm on workdays, 10:30am on Sun

La Zorra y El Cuervo *Jazz club attracting both established stars and emerging talents*
Calle 23, between Calle N and O, Vedado
@cubahavana.com/where-to-go/
la-zorra-y-el-cuervo
+53 7 8332402

Ludwig Foundation of Cuba *Talent pool for the next generation of Cuban artists*
Calle 13 N° 509, Vedado
@wiki/The_Ludwig_Foundation_of_Cuba
+53 7 8324270 / 7 8329128

Malecón 42 *Havana's famous waterfront*
Stretching 8 km from Old Havana's northern coast to the Almendares River in Vedado

Memorial José Marti *Memorial for one of Cuba's national heroes (1853–1895) and scenic viewpoint*
Plaza de la Revolución
@wiki/José_Martí_Memorial
+53 7 8820906
Mon–Fri, 9:00am–4:30pm

Mercado agropecuario *Best fruit and vegetable market in Havana*
Corner of Calle 19 and Calle B, Vedado
@onthegrid.city/havana/vedado/
agropecuario-19-b

Necrópolis de Cristóbal Colón *Largest cemetery in Latin America*
Main entrance at Calle Zapata, Vedado
@wikipedia.org/wiki/Colon_Cemetery, Havana

Playita 16 *Concrete beach with bar and restaurant, favored by locals*
Avenida 1, between Calle 14 and Calle 16, Miramar

Plaza Vieja 17 *One of the main colonial plazas in Old Havana with a high density of cozy cafes, bars, and thrilling art spaces*

Real Fábrica de Tabacos Partagás *Cigar factory and shop*
Calle San Carlos 816, corner of Calle Penalver, Centro Habana
@cigaraficionado.com/article/
the-new-partagas-factory-1899
+53 7 8620086

San Isidro, Merced, Acosta, and Picota 36
Hotspot for murals and graffiti in Old Havana

Tropicana *Open-air cabaret founded in 1939, with legendary dance performances*
Calle 72 A N° 4505, Marianao
@cabaret-tropicana.com
+53 7 2670110
Wed–Sun, 8:30pm–12:30am,
shows start at 10:00pm

INFO & TRANSPORTATION

Centro de Información Turística ℹ *Main location for tourist information*
Calle Obispo 524, Habana Vieja
@cubatravel.cu/destinos/la-habana
+53 7 8663333

Cubyke *Electric bike tours*
@cubyke.com
Avenida 7 N° 8607 c/o Ecotur, Miramar
+53 7 2144383 / 5 6080390

Estación Central de Ómnibus *Viazul buses depart from here to all parts of the country*
Avenida Independencia 101, corner of Calle 19 de Mayo, Plaza de la Revolución
@viazul.wetransp.com
+53 5 9890616 / 5 9890618 / 5 9890620

Velo Cuba *Bike rentals run by a women's collective*
Calle Obrapía 360, Habana Vieja, Cuba
@veloencuba.com
+53 5 2825148 / 7 8368820

Acknowledgements

I would like to thank Josephine Barbe, whose month-long upcycling workshop in Havana gave us the idea for this short book. The project owes its success to her enthusiasm and imagination as well as that of the designers—Alain, Ariadna, Aslin, Boris, Camila, Claudia, Dani, Deborah, Dorita, Madelaine, Monica, Nilse, and Urpi—who have been participating in the upcycling workshop HabanaTrapo and whose creations are published here for the first time.

Many thanks also go to Gysleda de la Barca and the participating models of Egos Agency for their grace and good humor.

A big thank you goes to the Oficina del Historiador (OHC, Historian's Office, www.portal.ohc.cu) of the City of Havana, who opened the doors and gates of Old Havana to us, especially Katia Cárdenas Jiménez, Taymi García Marichal, and Perla Rosales Aguirreurreta. I would also like to acknowledge the support of the Goethe-Institut, especially Lena Brode, Franziska Höfler, Verena Hütter, and Secretary General Johannes Ebert.

Our special thanks go to the team at Hirmer Publishers, especially Cordula Gielen, Lucia Ott, and publishing director Thomas Zuhr, as well as the copyeditor James Copeland, for their inspiring and professional collaboration.

For their personal commitment and participation, I would also like to thank Leire Fernandez and Idiana del Rio from Clandestina (www.nowinterisland.com), Alexandra Grömling from OXFAM Germany (www.fashionrevolution.org), Karla Batte, Norbert Flasch, Yaily Martínez Molina, Stephanie Pavlidis, Vanessa Sanchez, Karsten Schmitz and the Federkiel Foundation (www.federkiel.org), Rebecca Stoll, Erich Trefftz, and last but not least Ambassador Heidrun Tempel.

Michael M. Thoss

Authors

MT / **Michael M. Thoss** is a Hispanist and cultural scientist who, based in Havana, directed the Goethe-Institut offices for Cuba and the Caribbean from 2018 to the end of 2022.

BPV / **Boris Antonio Pérez Vázquez** is a fashion designer, artist, and curator of textile art. Since 2016, he has taught textile science at the State Institute of Industrial Design (ISDI) at the University of Havana.

AVM / **Arianet Valdívia Mesa** is a textile designer and professor at the State Institute of Industrial Design (ISDI) at the University of Havana, with a focus on innovation and management.

JB / **Josephine Barbe** is a fashion researcher and lecturer at the Technical University of Berlin, where she received her PhD. She has given several workshops on sustainable fashion design in Cuba, including at the State Institute of Industrial Design (ISDI) at the University of Havana. In 2022, she founded the HabanaTrapo project with thirteen Cuban designers.

RGM / **René Gutiérrez Mayrata** has been an architectural expert and historic preservationist at the Oficina del Historiador de la Ciudad de La Habana (Office of the City Historian of Havana) since 2006 and is involved in the restoration of Old Havana.

SPR / **Samuel Puente Rodríguez** is an architect and founding member of the collective Ad Urbis Arquitectos, which has received several international awards for its outstanding architectural projects. In 2022/23 he worked as curator of urbanism and industrial design at Fabrica de Arte in Havana.

COLOPHON

Concept and Idea
Michael M. Thoss and Hirmer Publishers

Project Management
Cordula Gielen, Hirmer Publishers

English Copyediting and Proofreading
James Copeland, Berlin

Graphic Design, Typesetting, and Production
Lucia Ott, Hirmer Publishers

Lithography and Prepress
Reproline mediateam GmbH & Co. KG,
Unterföhring

Paper
Garda Ultramatt 150 g/m^2

Printing and Binding
Grafisches Centrum Cuno GmbH & Co. KG,
Calbe (Saale)

Printed in Germany

*Bibliographic information published by the
Deutsche Nationalbibliothek*
The Deutsche Nationalbibliothek lists this
publication in the Deutsche Nationalbibliografie;
detailed bibliographic data are available online
at https://www.dnb.de.

© 2024 Hirmer Verlag GmbH, Munich, and the
authors
© 2023 VG Bild-Kunst, Bonn / Wifredo Lam
© Roberto Fabelo
© Alfredo Sosabravo

ISBN 978-3-7774-4267-9

www.hirmerpublishers.com

Cover image: Model Lisandra in a design by
Ariadna Doeste and Nilse Fonseca
Frontispiece: Model Deniye in a design by
Ariadna Doeste and Nilse Fonseca, as the duo
Yayaris

Image Credits

We have made every effort to identify copyright
holders. Any copyright owner who has been
inadvertently overlooked is asked to contact the
publisher. Justified claims will be settled in
accordance with the customary agreements.

All images: Claudia Rayment with support by
Rolando Cabrera, except:
p. 4: Carolina Álvarez
pp. 8–9: 100 files
p. 10: Justyna Serafín
pp. 11, 54, 68: AXP Photography
p. 12: © Pace Gallery, *Wifredo Lam: The
Imagination at Work*, 2022
p. 13: © Luciano Méndez, *Entre Lienzos
y escultura. Memorial José Martí*, 2018,
photo: Ricardo Elías and Rodolfo Martínez
p. 14: 100 files
p. 16: Anıl Karakaya
p. 18: © Beyond Roots, photo: Michael M. Thoss
pp. 20, 21, 50, 61 middle: Michael M. Thoss
p. 19: © Cris-Cris, photo: Claudia Raymant
p. 22: Mehmet Turgut Kirkgoz
p. 23: © Fábrica de Arte Cubano,
www.fabricadeartecubano.com
p. 25: latinsoul65/Flickr
pp. 28–29, 32–33 top: Matthias Oben
p. 30: Ryutaro Tsukata
pp. 51 top, 52, 53: Josephine Barbe
pp. 55–59: ArchivosRestauraOHC
p. 61 top: Loft Habana
pp. 62, 64, 65: Ad Urbis Arquitectos
p. 63: © Martínez-Becerra Arquitectos
pp. 66–67: © Alfredo Ramos and Katarzyna
Badach

Designers of the HabanaTrapo project
Camila Aguilar, Claudia Arcía, Aslin Asencio,
Ariadna Doeste, Nilse Fonseca, Monica García,
Daniela Hernández, Dora Jorrín, Alain Marzán,
Madelaine Muñoa, Boris Pérez, Urpi Rincón,
and Deborah Vázquez

(Contact via Boris Antonio Pérez Vázquez:
@borisantonioperez / +53 5 3241410)